Séance in Daylight

winner of the 2018 Frost Place Chapbook Competition

Séance in Daylight

poems

Yuki Tanaka

BULL★CITY
PRESS

DURHAM, NORTH CAROLINA

Séance in Daylight

Winner of the 2018 Frost Place Chapbook Competition
Selected by Sandra Lim

Library of Congress Cataloging-in-Publication Data
Tanaka, Yuki.
Séance in Daylight: poems / by Yuki Tanaka
p. cm.

ISBN-13: 978-1-4951-7882-5

Published in the United States of America

Book design by Spock and Associates

Cover art
Kansuke Yamamoto
A Chronicle of Drifting, 1949
Gelatin silver print collage, 30 × 24.8 cm
© Toshio Yamamoto
The J. Paul Getty Museum, Los Angeles

Published by
BULL CITY PRESS
1217 Odyssey Drive
Durham, NC 27713

www.BullCityPress.com

Table of Contents

Acknowledgements

The author would like to thank the editors of the following journals and anthologies, in which these poems first appeared:

American Poetry Review: "Homecoming," "Like One Who Has Mingled Freely with the World," "The Air Is an Exquisite Boneless Princess"

Denver Quarterly: "One Arm"

DIAGRAM: "Discourse on Vanishing"

Gulf Coast: "Prognosis at Midnight"

Kenyon Review: "Ghost in Waiting," "Evidence of Nocturne"

The Margins: "Séance in Daylight"

Poetry: "Death in Parentheses"

West Branch: "Exhibition of Desire," "The Empire of Light," "I Was Born in a Mountain Next to My Brother"

"Death in Parentheses" was reprinted in *Best New Poets 2017*.

...

I would like to thank my teachers, friends, family, and the Michener Center at UT-Austin for their encouragement and support. Thank you, Sandra Lim, for selecting my manuscript for the Frost Place Competition. I am grateful to the Frost Place and Bull City Press for making the publication of this chapbook possible.

Séance in Daylight

Homecoming

In the heart of a forest, a boy leans on
a light-lashed horse. He's not crying.
The horse unhurt, just as a husk
is unhurt. Lost in the forest, stroking

the frosted skin of its muscular neck,
he looks far ahead. Someone waiting.
He thinks, Make our journey last
a little longer. Say: it was a small

beautiful town. He was loved by friends.
No, he says, he had only the horse. Horse
made of white threads. Pull them out,
and the horse would lose its strength

and collapse into a man. The idea
is comforting. He could tell the horse,
who is now a man, he is tired
and cannot go on.

Like One Who Has Mingled Freely with the World

I cannot fly. I jump and jump to imitate a bird.
Surrounded by children, I leap up
with a huge silk scarf around my shoulders
to look like a crane. They laugh and laugh
and push me into a rabbit skin and watch.
At night I glint with long ears and peep through
a window misted with the steam from a tea kettle,
hoping that they'll let me in. I'm mostly alone.
They want to keep me as a legend:
invisible, silly, a hopeless woman-chaser.
That's what I was to the girl in a wedding kimono.
She screamed when I popped up from the rice paddy
like a big frog, sniffed her musk, aroused, and got
very tired. There's no harm in me except some
occasional cuts. They're meant to remind you of life.
Dirty, honest, lonely—if the sun was a pool
of red ink, I'd dive in and come out
beautiful, tanned, cancerous. Death
might cheer me up, make me feel
more human. Perched on a wooden fence,
I hold an umbrella up against the clear sky,
but no bird or animal falls from the sun.
It looks bigger than yesterday, like a bad sore
geese have pecked at over and over, and now
it's bulging, festering, ready to gush down
and drown us. I won't tell anyone about it. I wait.
It might drop some riches, some food, some wings.

Death in Parentheses

He came home with his right leg made a bit shorter
but they didn't notice. A landmine did it, he said
to himself, and I was the only one who heard him
because I followed him everywhere like a son.
He hobbled when no one was looking,
and I hobbled behind him.
When he plucked an iris, I plucked the one next to it,
and we thought of purple evening clouds.
When he killed a butterfly, he'd take off the wings first,
then crush it with his fingers and smell it.
I tried to catch one, but it flitted away.
He wanted to build a huge power plant
to keep us from disappearing. I nodded
and pointed out all the recent deaths, how quick they were,
tomatoes not as plump as they used to be,
the maple trees discolored, their branches
like veins with no fat around them.
All this, he decided, meant we needed new things.
But I disagreed on this: why new, why not
old me, I who have lived here for many years
even before he was born, but he didn't listen.
Mosquitoes come and go,
full and happy. Outside the window, the plant
looms over the village. It looks prettier than I thought,
which makes me want to kiss it, but I know it will
burn my lips and I won't be able to speak to anyone
with my charred mouth. I saw him

dressed up for a meeting, and they shouted,
blaming him for his empty head,
for wanting too much. The next time I saw him
he was in bed, old and delirious.
He opened his eyes, and held my hand
for the first time, and said, Don't push yourself, come back
alive. He was buried in his ever-vanishing land,
and I flew off into my friendless life.

The Air Is an Exquisite Boneless Princess

She waited for someone who wasn't like me.
If I stopped by her house, she'd stare
at the curtain's movement and dream of an ocean.
But no one else came. I tried to make her laugh
by hanging from the eaves, and she pushed me
back and forth like a swing
until my arms got tired. If I were a man
who could skip stones far enough, they'd reach
the other side of a lake, where she'd be standing.
I wore a bulky jacket to look bigger.
Once I built a ladder for her. When she started climbing,
it buckled and she fell, knocking me over.
She said, "I am the lightning, you are the tree,"
and put me back on my feet. She told me
a story she'd heard from her mariner lover
about lotus land: "Sea spray covers your skin with salt
and makes you glitter. There you eat red flowers
and forget everything. You turn into mist,
wetting and sucking robins' feathers, unnoticed
like a shy octopus." I liked that. On a stormy day,
I wore a loose shirt and let the wind pump up my chest
and laughed. She coughed, making the air move.

Exhibition of Desire

Would you like a slice of pear or a slice
of amethyst? It tastes of nightmare and we,

mice in silk kimonos, rustling across
a fragile bridge. Nearly identical, sick

of the vast, Midwestern sky, quiet as dry
starfish. Eyed, dipped in a basin, a beautiful

bundle of nerves. I remember
a harvest behind the curtain, that white

swollenness in the Spring Room: a throat
frosted to the bone, and then

the tremor of gelatin beneath the skin—
grass in the mouth, green breath in winter.

Then, the endless curiosity
of earth: a muddy river in the distance

saturated me as the soul lingers in the body
to feel its sinews unravel, raw—

my little island at war. A brazier warms
a windowful of eyes. There are no flowers like us,

patient or numbed. There is no hunger
like ours, seducers of scattered beauty.

Emptied of blazing organs, we flew lightly,
then pulled, sunk beneath, by wanting.

The Empire of Light

We are asked to stand at the pond. A sudden light
drowns us. Four empty turtles filled with flowers.

We use our bodies to grasp a foreign tongue.
Red-eyed fingers, porcelain skin, dark eyelashes

that never fall. Come, we say in unison, and they come
as ants gather around a slowly loosening sugar cube.

Here is a bowl to keep us whole. Here is a peacock fan
to cool our foreheads. On a rainy day,

we furnish our room with pink shells, pink imitation lips.
There is no ocean here. A stuffed bird on the mantel

has a calm look. Hunted in sleep, gutted,
the senses all dried up—thirst, terror. A fake crane

in the garden waits for spring. Droplets on the window
swarm over marigolds like blind bees.

The tip of my long hair can disturb the water
as squid ink overflows a delicate vial.

Soon I am going home. Changed, forgotten—
a girl in a barren field, pressing twilight to her throat.

I Was Born in a Mountain Next to My Brother

1.

Wolf skins kept us warm.
The cave yawned and swallowed
our cries for food. Our aunt came
to rescue us. Afraid for us
when we didn't sweat,
she gathered rain in a pail
and washed our bodies.
We had dimples and used them
to our benefit: she fed us milk,
bird, dog in a basket woven
like fingers praying for something.
Then it hailed. She said
that's a monster scuttling on the roof,
looking for you, so keep quiet.
We did, only to burst out laughing
when she left. There was a time
when a spider web was our shirt,
the moon a butterfly caught
in our retina. Now we are old
enough to be useful. While we work
a pine cone falls and cuts my skin.
Blood, isn't it, my brother says
and licks. Once, troubled by night,
we crawled through the mud

until our knees hit a buried wheel.
We thought it was the stairs
to a hidden room where our family
would be waiting with a bloodline.

2.

A man drowned in a river.
We scoop up the water
and look at his face. Inside
his egg-shaped head, a white
spasm—death looks like birth.
We chew a fat magnolia
and trudge forward, following
drumbeats from distant lanterns.
My brother is thin as a wet doll.
I stroke his back as mother would.
A birch sways like a stream
of sand, making us long for rain.
When we arrive at a village,
we see from behind the bush
a bonfire, men and women
dancing around it, a ruddy
sweaty circle, calling spirits
home. They all look well-fed.
They all look happy.
To join them, we must learn
their moves, the way
they submit to the rhythm.
We raise our arms
and step toward the light,

pushed by soft hands with the force
that rips the stem from petals.
We find ourselves in the center.

3.

They try to fatten us. I work
as a salt-maker, burning seaweed.
My brother sleeps on the barley mat.
The doctor says nothing is wrong
with his lungs, but his stomach
is very bad. He's getting thinner.
He's a cicada shell that lets in
too much light. What is his next body?
A blue azalea, a gull falling—
I might not recognize him once he's gone.
His eyes reflect my face. His breath,
thick as a moth, brushes my cheek.
At night I eat alone. When he wakes up,
he says he dreamed of our parents
in a warm house, and he was a butterfly
clinging to their window. When I hold
a bowl to his mouth, he shakes his head.
Pale face, pale fingers, salmon-red lips
trapped in moonlight. He's the more
beautiful of the two, and kinder.
The smoke of myrrh circles his pupils.
He's tired. He's dying into another life.

Seasonal Pleasure in the Time of War

A door clicks shut and we're invisible.
The floor is spotted like a hard freckled back

bearing animal after animal.
A gift of shale is already breaking.

Sugared peels to scrub the dead skin.
Though we were injured, we would say no.

Were we here or there—we would say no.
A caterpillar stiffens on the pane.

Winter will remove our lobes.
Street light helps us read: a boy with a satchel

sailing to an island, ghosts thrown off
in a bouquet. The ship will come back

and take us away. There's plenty of water left,
our fruit well preserved. Come, winter

of broad shoulders. Eyes of raisins, charcoal nose.
Tighten your cold hands around our thighs.

Ghost in Waiting

He watches me through the oleander bush.
The rain has softened his cigarette—

is he burning still. A jar of plums cools underground,
maturing the flesh. He lingers inside the flames,

his hair like weeds grasping a stone, the bones
breaking, until what's left is the scraped roof

of a mouth. Afterheat resists the morning chill.
Unshriveled. We are not separate.

His scent reddens the hour. The air thickens
as the smoke enters the room. I wish for a breeze

that animates my hair—I will not suffocate a bee.
Pollen over his bright chest. What grows from where

to what. Trapped heat. Dirt. Thick gauze
on a wound that heals and unheals in sweat.

Evidence of Nocturne

Whatever is singing above, come down.
Drink a lake from my eyes, fever and azaleas

both thriving on the shore.
Don't eat when your mouth is dry—

even a scrap of bread makes you bleed.
Withdraw. No lion devours the bones

of a beloved. Tonight, after rain
I'd like you to fly through these irises,

your blue mustache, blue cheeks
infected with sky. You can be frail here.

Between the clouds, a moonlit plane,
a thousand houses to be washed away.

This pile of wood wished to be a stairway
but couldn't. Will you pretend to climb it.

Séance in Daylight

She opened her mouth as if her throat were a bird
ready to leave her. I thought she was going to sing
for the dead, because she saw them always.
I was cold. I snuggled against her like a tall cat.
When she put the petals of a hydrangea on my eyelids,
I heard rain pattering behind them, and I was a window
from which she saw her friends return:
lights lit inside them, now alive, now burning,
moths in a struggle to escape their own wings
edged with fire. She waved at them
and spoke through me, fogging my skin with words
I couldn't hear. I wasn't cold anymore,
her breath so warm, her cheek pressed against
the fragile glass, which was my body.

One Arm

A bare white arm
disinfected. Plump, sizzling.
Should I let it speak, or just imagine
it speaks? Beauty

in a dustbin.
A panda in pantaloons.
The moon paisleyed on a doily.
Delicious disfigurement.

That arm
bared for the first time in the spring—
Whose arm? Blue perfume moistened
my mouth. A made thing.

As if I had forgotten how
hardtack stuck in the molars,
how I could not salivate for thirst.
As if I had forgotten

roofless stations, the burns.
A car's headlights skid through the mist
like hyperemic eyes.
Pigeons on the mezzanine

pulped to feathers. Laminated fairies
—made things. A letter from Mishima:
"House of the Sleeping Beauties" is "unusual
for formal perfection."

Like a frozen sparrow. The arm
peppered with antiseptics. Let it
speak. The pulse
of a detached arm.

The first sentence: "I can let you have
one of my arms for the night."
She tears her arm off
and places it on my knee.

Prognosis at Midnight

I listen to the moon but it doesn't say much about my life.
Quiet night is for my cockatoo. He keeps chattering
until my neighbor comes over to complain. Then I read
a local newspaper: no murder, no robbery, one grandmother
fell down the stairs and broke her hip. I lick my inky fingers
and order my imaginary chauffeur to get ready—I'll visit her
and comfort her. I'd say, I read about you, I'm terribly sorry,
this is my cockatoo, he's twelve and loves carrots.
We'd share her hospital dinner and be happy.
Other sick people gather around us, admiring my cockatoo,
who looks proud in his cage, unfurling his light-pink wings
like stage curtains, and I'm his assistant. Grandma,
worried that I've become silent, tells me how tired I look.
"I had a series of nightmares," I say, "my boss returned
from the grave and fired me, bats attacked me like slow bullets
but bigger, I was bleeding." She says: "When I'm alone,
I paint eyes on a pear and whisper, I'm watching over you."
That makes her stronger. Back home, my body thin and healthy,
cooling my feet on a crystal ball like a psychic out of business,
I look out the window: I don't know which leaves will fall first or why.
There aren't many trees left. Not much is left of this little town.

Discourse on Vanishing

1.

I will start with modern inventions: growth,

abundance, which brought out a world

filled with the dying. Nothing happens.

Children, echoing brooks, hard jaws yawning

in the background. Our place knows us,

our pulsations. This fleeting desire

to last longer, shadowed by clouds

that pass away as soon as we focus

on the sky. Broken ghost. The sun is cold

but does not come to an end. Stasis, deadlock.

Animate this landscape. There is no birdsong.

2.

Look at puppets performing this very act

with consciousness. The waves dilate

without order. Glutted heart. The waves,

claiming unity, unrelieved rhythm,

progress, breaking on shore.

                              She weaves

waves and light, remembering waves and birds.

The hand hidden behind the wool. She tries

to capture a blue flower as it vanishes

in a garden. Again and again. What seems to be

its murmur endures. Clipped murmur. Deep-blue

ripple: "He is dead," we stumble, "He is dead."

3.

This blue already fading beneath the waves

which threaten to encrust a diver. Mist

pouring into the body, formless, real

like a child. This new world at the end of pain

remains the same. The night descends

over houses. They are robbed of windows,

give out daylight. The darkness washing

the mist from the fields, grazing the eye.

Now, life can swerve, leaving the afterimage

of its absence: an old wine-bottle and behind it,

the arm of a woman, green sky flickering.

4.

The next landscape introduces a fire.

The fire is real. There is no speech.

When a boy collapses over the basin,

a dream comes, already posthumous:

sunken streets, valleys full of faces,

a young horse yearning for strength.

This is an end in view, beginning

over and over. People spring to life,

watching the breath of a wounded animal.

A faint chirping from somewhere—

unseen, forgotten cages.

5.

Her fever is difficult. She complains

about spots. The cold laughter of a man

who suffers in a burning dress.

Waltzes playing. Uncontrollable laughter.

A Salome dances, replaced by another

in quick succession, confused.

The night falls flat in a crowded room.

The woman tries to talk, unable to turn her eyes

from a body struck outside. Bright light—

no more. The earth stays still again.

This is not the end of the broken world.

Notes

"Like One Who Has Mingled Freely with the World" was inspired by *Kamaitachi* (1969), a book of photographs by Japanese avant-garde photographer Eikoh Hosoe.

The title "The Air Is an Exquisite Boneless Princess" is adapted from a poem by Shuzo Takiguchi, called "Document d'Oiseaux: Official Report on Birds," which I co-translated with Mary Jo Bang. Our translation appeared on the *Boston Review* website for the 2015 National Poetry Month.

"Exhibition of Desire" and "The Empire of Light" were inspired by photographs of Japanese women who had come to St. Louis as part of the Japanese exhibition for the 1904 World's Fair. The second poem was named after a series of paintings by René Magritte.

"One Arm" is based on the short story of the same title by Japanese novelist Yasunari Kawabata. The line "I can let you have…" is adapted from Edward Seidensticker's translation of the story.

"Prognosis at Midnight" borrows its cockatoo and newspaper from Joseph Cornell's *For Juan Gris #7* (1954).

"Discourse on Vanishing" is an erasure of the first half of my doctoral dissertation "Tempo and Temporality in Anglo-American Modernist Literature." The poem draws on the language of Virginia Woolf's *The Waves* and Djuna Barnes's *Nightwood*.

About the Author

Yuki Tanaka was born and raised in Yamaguchi, Japan. He is an MFA student at the Michener Center for Writers at the University of Texas-Austin. His poems have appeared in *American Poetry Review*, *Best New Poets*, *Kenyon Review*, *Poetry*, and elsewhere. His translations of modern Japanese poetry (with Mary Jo Bang) have appeared in *New Republic*, *Paris Review*, and *A Public Space*, among other journals.